Contents

All Kinds of Plants

There are many different plants.
They grow in different shapes and sizes.
They grow all around the world.

Some plants are very large.

Some plants are very small.

▲ The buttercup is a small yellow **flower** that grows in Europe.

▲ The giant redwood is a very large tree that grows in the USA.

Some plants are very tall.

◀ Bamboo is a tall grass that grows in Asia.

Some plants are very prickly.

▼ The cactus is a prickly plant that grows in deserts.

Can you find any large, small, tall or prickly plants near where you live?

Plants with Flowers

Lots of plants grow **flowers**.
They are called flowering plants.

▲ A fruit tree grows many flowers in the
spring. They are called **blossom**.

flower

petal

stem

leaf

Some plants grow just one flower.

A poppy has red **petals**.

Seeds are made in flowers.

New poppy plants grow from poppy seeds.

Go for a walk in the spring or summer. How many different flowers can you see? What colours are the petals?

Plants with Cones

Some plants have **cones** instead of **flowers**. **Seeds** are made inside the cones.

Cones grow on trees called conifers.

◄ This conifer is a pine tree.

Pine trees grow in cold places where there is often snow. They grow lots of cones.

Cones have scales.
They protect the seeds.

New pine trees grow from a seed.

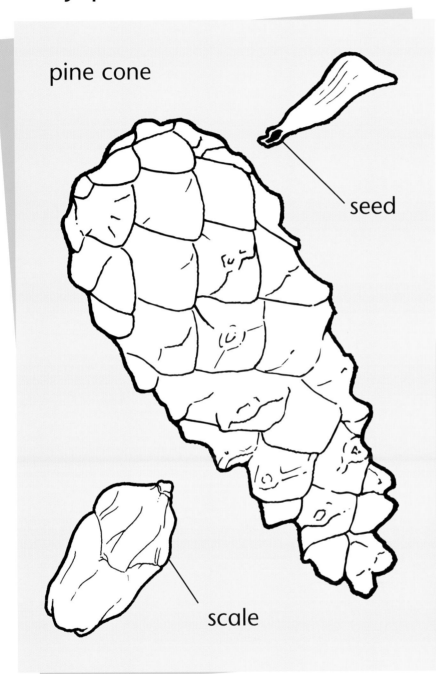

pine cone

seed

scale

▲ A pine cone

Conifers grow where it snows. How do you think their hard pointy cones help to protect the seeds from the snow?

Plants without Flowers or Cones

Some plants do not grow **flowers** or **cones**.

◀ Bladder wrack is a seaweed. Air bubbles in its **fronds** help the plant float in water.

Seaweed and ferns grow **spores**. The spores form on the plants' fronds, which are like **leaves**.

Ferns usually grow in woods. A fern makes thousands of tiny spores under its fronds.

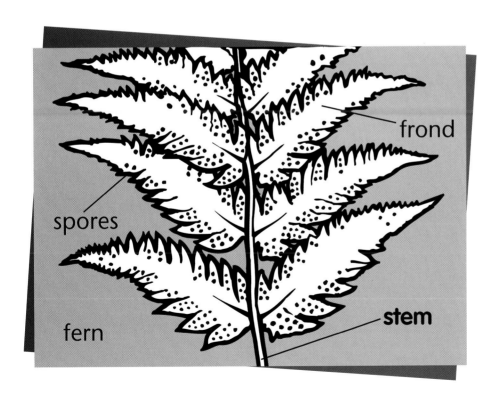

frond

spores

fern

stem

New ferns grow from the spores.

Next time you walk on the beach or in the woods, look out for seaweeds or ferns.

Food Makers

Plants need food to stay alive, just like us. They don't eat food, they make it inside their **leaves**.

Most plants have green leaves.

◀ A cabbage makes its food in its green leaves.

Leaves contain green colouring called **chlorophyll**. Chlorophyll works with water, air and sunlight to make the plant's food.

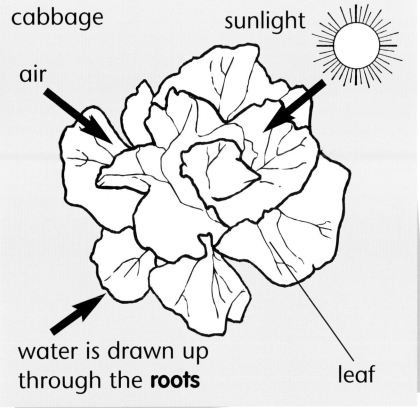

cabbage

air

sunlight

water is drawn up through the **roots**

leaf

Take a walk outside. Look at the leaves of different plants. How many of them are green?

Plants as Food

Plants are very important because animals, including us, need them as food.

▲ Cows eat grass.

▲ **Fruits**, **vegetables**, bread, pasta and breakfast cereals all come from plants.

We eat lots of different **seeds** called **grains**. Rice, wheat, oats and barley are all grains.

◀ This is wheat grain. It is used to make bread.

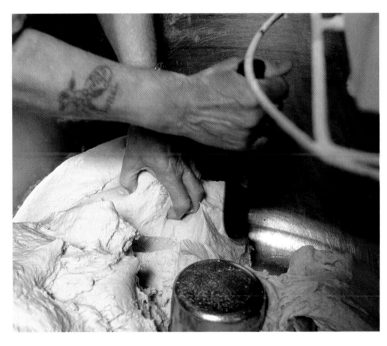

▲ Bread dough

Grain is ground into flour. This is mixed with water and **yeast** to make dough. The dough is baked into bread.

Next time you go shopping, have a look at some foods. Can you tell which come from plants?

Fruits and Vegetables

Fruits and **vegetables** come from different parts of a plant.

Fruits grow from the **flowers** of a plant. They have **seeds** inside them that will grow into new plants.

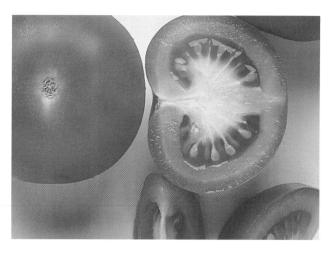

▲ These are all fruits because they have seeds inside them. Even a tomato is a fruit.

We can eat other parts of a plant. They are called vegetables.

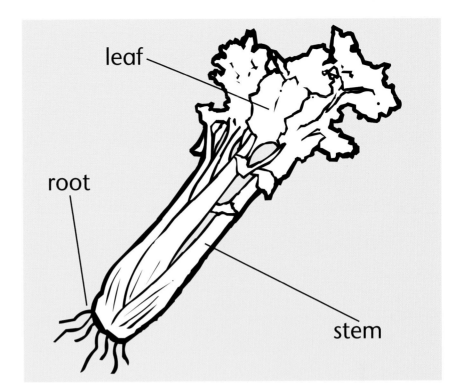

leaf

root

stem

▶ Celery plant

▲ We eat the **leaves** of a cabbage plant.

▲ We eat the **stem** of a celery plant.

▲ We eat the **root** of a carrot plant.

What other vegetables can you think of?
Are they the leaves, stems or roots of a plant?

Poisonous Plants

Some plants can make us ill because they are **poisonous**.

▲ When we eat rhubarb we eat the **stem** of the plant. Rhubarb **leaves** are poisonous to us.

▶ These are the **flowers** of a laburnum tree. Its flowers, **seeds,** leaves and **roots** will all make us ill.

Mushrooms and toadstools
can be very poisonous.

Although mushrooms and toadstools
are not plants (they are called **fungi**)
they grow next to plants. You can find
them in lawns and in woods.

 When you touch plants or fungi you
should always wash your hands
afterwards. You should never put
plants in your mouth unless you
know they are safe.

Useful Plants

We use plants in many different ways. Cotton, rubber and some medicines are made from plants.

◀Cotton plants have green **fruits** that split open. Inside are **seeds** and white fibres.

▶ Cotton fibres are picked from the cotton plant. They are pulled out into long thin threads and then woven into cloth.

Rubber comes from the liquid or **sap** inside a rubber tree.

◀ The liquid is called **latex**. It is used to make things such as car tyres.

Plants are also used in medicines. Aspirin is made from the **bark** of a willow tree. Aspirin helps to make us better when we have colds or headaches.

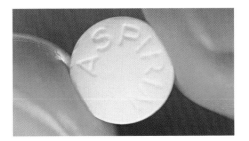

Many shampoos and soaps are made using plants, such as coconut. Have a look at some labels and see what plants are in the ingredients.

Trees and Wood

Trees are plants. The trunk and branches of trees are made from wood. Wood is very useful.

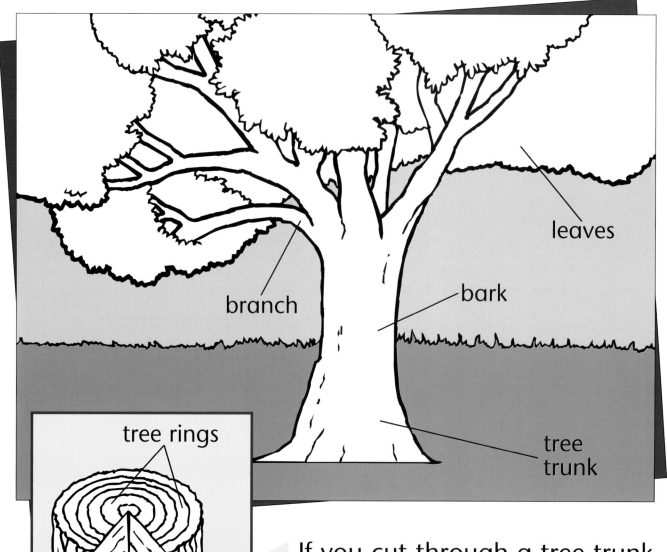

leaves

branch

bark

tree rings

tree trunk

wood   bark

◀ If you cut through a tree trunk and count the number of rings, you can tell the age of the tree. Each ring is one year of growth.

Wood is hard and can be cut into different shapes. It can be made into many things.

◀ This house is made of wood.

Have a look around your house. What can you find that is made of wood?

Looking after Plants

Plants are very useful.
They provide food and shelter for
people and animals. We need
to look after plants.

▲ In our gardens and parks we look
after plants by making sure that they
have enough light and water.

The **rainforests** are large tropical forests. They are hot and wet all year round.

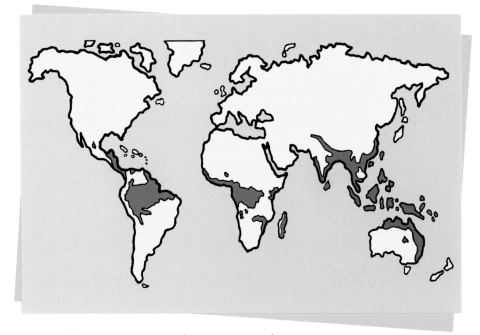

▲ This map shows where rainforests grow in the world.

Rainforests are home to many plants, birds, animals and people. We need to look after their forest home and not chop too much of it down.

Amazing Plants

The longest seaweed, the Pacific giant kelp, can be 60 metres long. It can grow about 45 cm in one day.

The biggest tree in the world is the Giant Sequoia. It can grow to over 79 metres tall and be as wide as 24 metres. Sequoias are found in California, USA.

The Douglas fir tree can grow to be over 126 metres tall. One of the tallest was found in Columbia, Canada.

Use this book to find the answers to this Amazing Plants quiz!

- What kind of plant is a bamboo?

- Where are seeds made in most plants?

- On what type of trees can you find cones?

- Name two types of plants that have fronds instead of leaves.

- Where do plants make their food?

- What part of a cabbage plant do we eat?

- What part of a rhubarb plant is poisonous?

- How can you tell the age of a tree?

Glossary

bark   tough material that covers the outside of trees.

blossom   flowers that grow on fruit trees.

chlorophyll   green colouring found in leaves and fronds.

cone   type of fruit that is found on conifer trees.

flower   part of a plant that is usually very colourful. The flower becomes the fruits and seeds of a flowering plant.

fronds   leaf like part of some plants where spores grow.

fruit   part of a plant that grows from the flower and protects the seed or seeds.

fungi   a group of living things including mushrooms, toadstools and yeast that grow on other living things. One of the group on its own is called a fungus.

grains   cereal plants that are grown for foods.

latex   milky liquid or sap that comes from the rubber tree.

leaf   part of a plant that is usually green. The leaf uses sunlight, air and water to make food for the plant.

petals   outer parts of a flower that are often colourful.

poisonous   something that will make you ill if you eat or touch it.

rainforests   large, thick forests that grow in hot, damp places.

root   part of a plant that holds the plant in the soil. The roots take up water from the soil.

sap   milky liquid found inside plants.

seed   seeds are made in the flower of a flowering plant. When seeds are planted new plants grow from them.

spore   spores are made under the leaves of ferns and seaweed. New plants grow from spores.

stem   part of a plant that holds up the leaves and flowers. The stem carries water from the roots to the leaves.

vegetable   part of a plant that is not the fruit, such as the flower, stem, leaf or root.

yeast   type of fungus used to make bread.

Index

30